Cartoons & Me

1, Volume 1

LEONARD KISAU

Published by LEONARD KISAU, 2024.

While every precaution has been taken in the preparation of this book, the publisher assumes no responsibility for errors or omissions, or for damages resulting from the use of the information contained herein.

CARTOONS & ME

First edition. September 8, 2024.

ISBN: 979-8227963482

Written by LEONARD KISAU.

Also by LEONARD KISAU

1
Best Online Ventures in 2024
Raising Girls
Sandy Beaches of Africa
Cartoons & Me

Watch for more at https://www.familymedia.com.

This book is dedicated to my wonderful girls, whose boundless curiosity and imagination continually inspire me. May you always find joy in the simple wonders of life, like the colorful world of cartoons, where anything is possible and dreams take flight. As you grow, may you carry with you the lessons of kindness, courage, and creativity that these stories teach, and may your lives be filled with adventure, laughter, and love. This is for you, my shining stars.

CARTOONS AND ME

CHAPTER 1: THE WORLD OF CARTOONS

Timmy was an ordinary boy with an extraordinary love for cartoons. Every morning, he would rush downstairs in his pajamas, his bowl of cereal in hand, and turn on the TV to watch his favorite cartoon shows. He had a special routine—first *Super Paws*, then *Galactic Warriors*, and finally *Jungle Rangers*. It didn't matter how many times he had seen the episodes; he never got bored of them. Timmy would laugh out loud at the funny parts and sit on the edge of his seat when the heroes faced danger. To him, cartoons were not just entertainment—they were his window to a world where anything was possible. He felt like cartoons were speaking directly to him, filling his life with joy and excitement.

Among all the shows Timmy watched, *Super Paws* was his absolute favorite. The main character, Captain Paws, was a brave and clever dog with the power to fly and save the day. Timmy loved how Captain Paws used his superpowers to defeat the villains and protect the town. There was also Kitty Claw, a sneaky yet kind-hearted cat with super speed, and Bruno, a strong bear who could talk to animals. Timmy had action figures of all of them and would often act out the episodes, pretending to be Captain Paws himself. Sometimes, he would tie a towel around his shoulders like a cape and run around the house, shouting, "I'm coming to the rescue!" His mom would laugh, but she knew that in Timmy's mind, he was really part of the cartoon.

Timmy's imagination knew no bounds when it came to cartoons. During lunchtime, his sandwich would turn into a spaceship, and his apple would be a tiny planet waiting to be explored by Captain Paws and his team. At the park, Timmy would swing as high as he could, imagining that he was flying through the sky, just like his cartoon heroes. His best friend, Sarah, loved playing along with him. She would pretend to be Kitty Claw, zooming around the playground with her "super speed."

Together, they would save the world from invisible villains and make up new adventures. For Timmy, the line between the real world and the cartoon world was very thin. Cartoons made everything around him more magical.

Each night, after watching his favorite shows, Timmy would lie in bed, staring at the glow-in-the-dark stars on his ceiling. He would close his eyes and imagine what it would be like to actually live in a cartoon. In his dreams, he could fly through the sky, talk to animals, and battle evil villains with his superpowers. The colors would be brighter, the characters funnier, and the adventures more exciting than anything in the real world. "If only I could be part of a cartoon," Timmy would think to himself as he drifted off to sleep. In his heart, he believed that being inside a cartoon would be the greatest adventure ever.

One ordinary afternoon, something extraordinary happened that would change Timmy's life forever. He was sitting on the couch, watching an episode of *Super Paws*, when the screen began to flicker. Timmy blinked, thinking it was just a glitch, but then the TV started to glow with a strange, magical light. The glow grew brighter and brighter until it filled the entire room, and before Timmy could react, he felt a powerful force pulling him towards the screen. "What's happening?" he shouted, grabbing onto the couch, but it was too late. In a flash of light, Timmy was sucked into the TV and found himself standing in the middle of the cartoon world. His dream had come true—but was he ready for the adventure that awaited him?

Timmy could hardly believe his eyes as he stood in the middle of Cartoon Land. Everything around him was bursting with color—trees with bright purple leaves, houses shaped like giant ice cream cones, and characters he had only seen on TV walking down the streets. His heart raced with excitement. "This can't be real," he whispered, looking at his hands. They weren't normal hands anymore—they looked just like cartoon hands, with bold outlines and bright colors! Timmy had become a cartoon character. He spun around in circles, laughing and jumping with joy. This was better than any dream he had ever had.

As Timmy looked around in amazement, a familiar voice called out, "Hey, Timmy! Over here!" He turned to see none other than Captain Paws flying toward him, cape flapping in the wind. Timmy's eyes widened in disbelief. "Captain Paws? Is that really you?" he asked. The superhero dog landed gracefully beside him and gave him a big, friendly grin. "Of course, it's me! Welcome to Cartoon Land, kid!" Timmy's heart felt like it might explode from happiness. His hero was real, and he was talking to him! "I can't believe this!" Timmy said, his voice filled with excitement. Captain Paws chuckled. "Well, believe it, because the adventure is just beginning."

Captain Paws introduced Timmy to the rest of the *Super Paws* team—Kitty Claw, who zoomed over with her super speed, and Bruno, the talking bear who gave Timmy a big, gentle hug. "Welcome to our world," Bruno said in his deep, kind voice. Timmy couldn't stop smiling as he shook hands with all his favorite characters. "I've watched all of your episodes! I know all of your adventures!" Timmy exclaimed. Kitty Claw winked at him. "Well, now it's your turn to go on an adventure with us." Timmy's eyes lit up. "Wait, you mean I get to be part of the team?" he asked, hardly able to believe it. Captain Paws nodded. "That's right, kid. And we've got a mission for you."

Timmy's excitement turned into curiosity as Captain Paws led him to the *Super Paws* headquarters—a giant, futuristic building with gadgets and gizmos everywhere. "Our world is full of amazing adventures," Captain Paws explained as they walked through the glowing halls. "But sometimes, things go wrong, and that's where we come in." Timmy listened closely, eager to hear what kind of mission they had in store. "There's been some strange activity in the neighboring town of Bubble City," Captain Paws continued. "We need your help to figure out what's going on." Timmy's heart raced. He had always dreamed of being a hero, and now he had the chance to help save Cartoon Land.

The team gathered in the control room, where a large screen showed a map of Cartoon Land. "Bubble City is known for its floating buildings and bubbly characters," Captain Paws explained, pointing at the map. "But lately, the bubbles have been popping too quickly, and no one knows why." Timmy furrowed his brow, thinking hard. "That sounds serious. What do you think is causing it?" he asked. Bruno scratched his head. "We're not sure yet, but we think it might have something to do with a villain named Dr. Popper. He's been causing trouble in other parts of Cartoon Land, and we think he's behind this, too." Timmy clenched his fists, feeling a surge of determination. "Let's stop him!"

As they prepared for their mission, Timmy was given his very own superhero suit. It was blue with lightning bolts on the sides and a cape that fluttered behind him when he moved. "Wow, I look awesome!" Timmy said, admiring his reflection in the mirror. Captain Paws smiled. "You're officially part of the team now. Welcome aboard, Timmy." Timmy beamed with pride. He had always imagined what it would be like to wear a superhero suit, and now it was real! He couldn't wait to take on the adventure that lay ahead. "Let's do this!" he said, full of energy.

The team hopped into the *Super Paws* jet, which zoomed through the cartoon sky at lightning speed. As they soared above the colorful landscape, Timmy stared out the window in awe. He could see the different parts of Cartoon Land—Candy Mountain, where everything was made of sweets, Robot Valley, where robots of all shapes and sizes lived, and Bubble City, where giant bubbles floated gently in the air. "Look, there it is!" Kitty Claw shouted, pointing ahead. Timmy's eyes widened as they approached Bubble City. The buildings were floating in giant bubbles, just like on the TV show, but something was wrong. The bubbles were popping left and right, and the buildings were starting to wobble. "We need to act fast," Captain Paws said, his voice serious.

The jet landed in the middle of Bubble City, and Timmy jumped out, ready for action. As they walked through the streets, Timmy noticed that the bubble people looked worried. "What's happening here?" Timmy asked one of the bubble citizens. "Our bubbles are popping too quickly!" the bubble man replied. "If this keeps up, our whole city will fall apart!" Timmy frowned, determined to help. Captain Paws turned to the team. "We need to find Dr. Popper and stop him before it's too late," he said. Timmy nodded, feeling brave and ready to face whatever challenge came next.

As they searched the city, Timmy spotted something suspicious—a trail of popped bubbles leading toward a dark alley. "Look! Over there!" he shouted, pointing at the trail. The team followed the trail until they reached a hidden lair at the edge of the city. Inside, they found Dr. Popper, a sneaky villain with a giant pin that he used to pop bubbles. "Aha! I knew you would come," Dr. Popper sneered as he twirled his pin. "But you're too late! Bubble City will be destroyed!" Timmy clenched his fists. "Not if we can stop you!" he declared. Captain Paws growled, ready for action. It was time for Timmy and the *Super Paws* to save the day.

A fierce battle broke out as Dr. Popper tried to pop the bubbles faster than the team could save them. Timmy, using his new flying powers, soared through the sky, catching falling buildings and rescuing the bubble citizens. Captain Paws and Kitty Claw worked together to disarm Dr. Popper, while Bruno used his strength to rebuild the popped bubbles. Timmy felt like a true hero as he darted through the air, determined to protect the city. "You're not getting away with this, Dr. Popper!" Timmy shouted as he swooped down to grab the villain's pin. With a swift move, he knocked the pin out of Dr. Popper's hand, and the villain stumbled back in shock.

Dr. Popper tried to make a run for it, but Timmy and the team were too quick. Captain Paws tackled him to the ground, and Kitty Claw used her super speed to tie him up with a bubble rope. "You're finished, Dr. Popper!" Captain Paws declared, and the villain grumbled in defeat. The bubble citizens cheered as the team saved the city from collapse. Timmy felt a rush of pride as he looked around at the smiling faces. "We did it!" he shouted, high-fiving Kitty Claw. "You were amazing out there, Timmy," Captain Paws said with a grin. "You're a real hero." Timmy beamed. He had dreamed of being part of a cartoon, and now he had saved an entire city. It was the best day of his life.

After the battle, the team returned to the *Super Paws* headquarters, where they celebrated their victory with a feast of cartoon food—giant ice cream cones, floating pizzas, and candy that changed colors when you ate it. Timmy couldn't stop smiling as he sat with his new friends. "I still can't believe I'm really here," he said, taking a bite of his floating pizza. Captain Paws chuckled. "Believe it, kid. You've earned your place here." As the night went on, Timmy felt more at home in Cartoon Land than ever before. He had become part of the cartoon world, just like he had always dreamed. And this was only the beginning of his incredible adventures.

CHAPTER 2: A NEW CARTOON ADVENTURE

Timmy stood in the middle of the cartoon world, still in awe of everything around him. The sky was a vibrant shade of pink, with clouds shaped like animals bouncing playfully above. The grass under his feet was soft, almost like a carpet, and the trees were tall with colorful leaves that shimmered in the sunlight. Everywhere he looked, there were creatures and characters from all kinds of cartoons, walking, talking, and going about their day as if it was completely normal. Timmy blinked a few times to make sure he wasn't dreaming. "Am I really here?" he whispered to himself. But before he could think too hard, a voice interrupted him.

"Hey, kid! Over here!" Timmy turned to see a small, scruffy dog standing on two legs, waving a paw in his direction. The dog was wearing a bright yellow bowtie and had the friendliest face Timmy had ever seen. "I'm Bingo!" the dog barked cheerfully. "You must be new around here. Welcome to Cartoon Land!" Timmy's jaw dropped. "A talking dog?" he exclaimed. Bingo laughed and did a little dance on his hind legs. "Yep! We've got all kinds of fun stuff around here. You'll get used to it!" Timmy grinned, feeling a surge of excitement. "I can't believe this is happening," he said. "I've always dreamed of being in a cartoon."

Bingo quickly became Timmy's guide through Cartoon Town, the heart of Cartoon Land. The town was bustling with activity. There were buildings shaped like giant crayons, streets made of rubber, and every character seemed to be zipping around on hoverboards or flying with capes. "Come on, Timmy, let me show you around," Bingo said, leading the way. As they walked, Timmy's eyes were wide with wonder. There were all sorts of cartoon characters—giant robots playing hopscotch, friendly monsters selling ice cream, and a group of superheroes flying over the town square. "This place is amazing!" Timmy said. Bingo nodded. "It sure is! And the best part is, anything can happen here."

Timmy's excitement grew with every step. He felt like he was walking through one of his favorite shows, only this time he was part of it. "So, what do you do here, Bingo?" Timmy asked, curious about how things worked in Cartoon Land. Bingo scratched his ear with a paw. "Oh, I'm just your average talking dog. But everyone here has something special about them. You'll see soon enough!" Timmy's mind was racing. Everyone had something special? What could his special thing be? He had always imagined having superpowers, just like the characters in his favorite shows. "Do you think I could have a superpower?" Timmy asked, excitement bubbling inside him.

Bingo grinned. "Of course you do! Everyone in Cartoon Land has a superpower—it's just a matter of discovering what yours is." Timmy's eyes widened. A superpower? Him? The thought was thrilling. "But how do I find out what my power is?" he asked, eager to begin. Bingo wagged his tail. "That's where the School of Superpowers comes in. It's where new characters like you go to learn all about their abilities and figure out what makes them special." Timmy's heart pounded with excitement. "A school for superpowers? That sounds awesome!" Bingo nodded. "And lucky for you, the school is just around the corner. Let's go check it out!"

As they walked through the town, Timmy couldn't stop thinking about what his superpower might be. "Maybe I'll be able to fly," he said out loud, imagining himself soaring through the sky like a superhero. "Or maybe I'll have super strength, and I'll be able to lift up cars and buildings!" Bingo chuckled. "You never know, Timmy. The possibilities are endless in Cartoon Land." Timmy grinned, daydreaming about all the amazing things he could do once he discovered his power. The more he thought about it, the more excited he became. "I can't wait to find out what my power is!" he said, practically bouncing with energy.

When they arrived at the School of Superpowers, Timmy's jaw dropped once again. The building was enormous, with tall, twisting towers and doors that sparkled with magic. A sign above the entrance read, "Welcome to the School of Superpowers: Unleash Your Inner Hero!" Timmy stared at the building in awe. "This place is incredible!" he exclaimed. Bingo nodded proudly. "This is where the magic happens. Inside, you'll meet all kinds of characters, and you'll get to train with the best superheroes in Cartoon Land." Timmy's heart raced as they walked up the steps. He was about to start the most exciting adventure of his life.

As they entered the school, Timmy felt like he had stepped into a whole new world. The hallways were filled with floating books, talking animals, and students practicing their powers. One student was turning invisible, while another was creating bursts of fireworks with a wave of her hand. Timmy's eyes were as wide as saucers. "This is amazing!" he whispered. Bingo led him to a large room with a stage in the center. "This is where new students get introduced," Bingo explained. "You'll be called up soon to start your training." Timmy's stomach did a flip. He was excited, but also a little nervous. What if he didn't have a cool power?

While waiting, Timmy watched as other students went up on stage. One by one, they discovered their powers—flying, super speed, shape-shifting, and even talking to animals. Timmy's heart raced as his turn got closer. "What if my power is something boring?" he whispered to Bingo. But Bingo gave him a reassuring smile. "Don't worry, Timmy. Everyone's power is special in its own way. You'll see." Timmy nodded, feeling a little better, but the butterflies in his stomach wouldn't go away. When his name was finally called, Timmy took a deep breath and stepped onto the stage, ready to discover what made him special.

Standing in the spotlight, Timmy felt a strange energy surge through him. The crowd was silent, waiting to see what would happen. Suddenly, Timmy felt light as a feather, and before he knew it, he was floating above the stage! "Whoa!" he gasped, looking down at the amazed faces below. "I'm flying!" The crowd erupted into cheers, and Timmy grinned from ear to ear. His dream had come true—he had the power to fly! He soared higher and higher, looping through the air with joy. "This is amazing!"

Timmy shouted, feeling the wind in his hair. His heart swelled with pride. He had a superpower, and it was better than anything he had ever imagined.

After discovering his power, Timmy couldn't wait to start his training. The School of Superpowers was full of teachers who specialized in helping students master their abilities. Timmy's flying instructor, a wise old owl named Professor Flap, taught him how to control his flight and perform tricks in the air. "Flying isn't just about speed," Professor Flap said during their first lesson. "It's about grace and control." Timmy listened carefully, determined to become the best flyer in Cartoon Land. Every day, he practiced soaring through the skies, dodging obstacles, and doing flips. With each lesson, he got better and better.

Timmy quickly became one of the top students in his class, and his new friends were amazed by his flying skills. "You're like a superhero!" one of them said. Timmy blushed, but inside he felt proud. He had come a long way from being just a regular boy watching cartoons. Now, he was living the adventure of a lifetime, and every day brought something new and exciting. As he zoomed through the air, Timmy couldn't help but think about how incredible it was to be in Cartoon Land. He had a superpower, amazing friends like Bingo, and the chance to explore a world full of magic and wonder.

But Timmy knew that this was just the beginning of his adventure. There was so much more to learn, and so many more places to explore in Cartoon Land. With Bingo by his side and the School of Superpowers to guide him, Timmy felt ready to take on any challenge. He had discovered his unique power, but now it was time to use it for something even bigger. "I can't wait to see what happens next," Timmy thought as he soared through the sky, leaving a trail of stardust behind him. Cartoon Land had become his new home, and every day was a new adventure waiting to unfold.

CHAPTER 3: DISCOVERING SUPERPOWERS

Timmy woke up early on his first day at the School of Superpowers, buzzing with excitement and nerves. His room was decorated with posters of his favorite cartoon characters, but this time, they felt different—he was now one of them, living in a world where anything was possible. As he got dressed in his new school uniform, he wondered what the day would bring. Would he make friends? Would he find his superpower? His stomach was a swirl of butterflies as he thought about meeting other students, each with their own special abilities. "This is it," Timmy whispered to himself. "Today's the day I become a hero."

When Timmy arrived at the school, he was greeted by a dazzling display of colors and sounds. The halls were filled with characters from all sorts of cartoons—some he recognized, and others he had never seen before. There was a superhero cat with laser eyes, a tiny dragon who could grow giant, and even a talking pencil that could draw anything into existence. Timmy couldn't believe his eyes. "Whoa, this is so cool!" he said, looking around in awe. He felt like he had stepped into one of his favorite cartoon episodes, but this time, he wasn't just watching—he was part of the action.

As Timmy walked through the grand doors of the school's main hall, he saw other students gathering for their first day of classes. There was a sense of excitement in the air as everyone talked about their powers. "I can control fire!" said one student proudly, flames dancing on his fingertips. "Well, I can turn invisible," another girl bragged, vanishing before their eyes. Timmy listened in awe, but deep down, he felt a little nervous. What if he didn't have a cool power like everyone else? He had dreamed of being a superhero for as long as he could remember, but now that he was here, the pressure was on.

Their first class was an introduction to superpowers, and the teacher, Professor Sparx, was a tall, glowing figure who could manipulate electricity. He stood at the front of the room, his hands crackling with energy as he spoke. "Welcome to the School of Superpowers," he said, his voice booming. "Here, you will discover your unique abilities and learn how to use them to make Cartoon Land an even better place. But remember—every power, no matter how big or small, is important." Timmy sat up straight, listening intently. He couldn't wait to find out what his power was, but at the same time, the idea of not knowing filled him with doubt.

During the class, Professor Sparx explained the different types of superpowers. There were elemental powers, like fire, water, and air, and there were transformation powers, like shape-shifting and invisibility. Some students had mind-based powers, like telepathy or controlling objects with their thoughts, while others had physical abilities like super strength or super speed. As Timmy listened, he couldn't help but wonder where he would fit in. Would he have an elemental power? Or maybe something completely different? The possibilities were endless, but that only made the mystery more nerve-wracking. He wanted to know now—what would his superpower be?

After the lesson, the students were taken to a special room called the Crystal Chamber, where they would discover their powers. Timmy's heart pounded as they entered the chamber. It was a vast, magical space filled with shimmering crystals of all colors, each one glowing softly. In the center of the room stood a giant crystal, as tall as a building, radiating energy. "This is the Power Crystal," Professor Sparx explained. "It reveals the unique ability within each of you. One by one, you will step forward and touch the crystal. When you do, your power will be revealed." Timmy's palms were sweaty as he stared at the crystal, wondering what it would show him.

Timmy watched as the other students stepped forward, one by one. Each time a student touched the crystal, a burst of light filled the room, and their power was revealed. One boy was surrounded by water, his power to control the ocean. Another girl was lifted into the air by an invisible force—she could control gravity! Timmy's heart raced faster with every student. Soon, it would be his turn. "I hope I don't have a boring power," he thought, his nerves growing. But then, it was his name being called. "Timmy, step forward," Professor Sparx said. Timmy took a deep breath and walked toward the crystal, his hands trembling with anticipation.

With shaky hands, Timmy reached out and touched the crystal. The moment his fingers made contact, he felt a surge of energy pulse through his body. His heart skipped a beat as the crystal began to glow brighter and brighter, filling the room with light. Suddenly, Timmy felt weightless. Before he knew it, his feet lifted off the ground, and he was floating in mid-air! "I'm flying!" he gasped, looking down at the amazed faces of his classmates. He couldn't believe it—his power was the ability to fly! The crystal's glow faded, and Timmy slowly floated back down to the ground, his heart pounding with excitement.

The room erupted into cheers as Timmy's classmates congratulated him. "That's so cool!" one of them said. "I wish I could fly!" Timmy grinned from ear to ear, feeling a rush of pride. He had always dreamed of flying, and now it was real. He could soar through the skies just like the superheroes he admired. "Well done, Timmy," Professor Sparx said with a smile. "Flying is a rare and special power. You'll need to train hard to master it, but I'm sure you'll do great." Timmy nodded, his excitement growing with each passing moment. He couldn't wait to try out his new ability.

Later that day, Timmy had his first flying lesson with Professor Flap, the wise old owl who taught all the flying students. They went to the Flight Fields, a wide-open space filled with floating platforms and obstacles for practicing. "The key to flying," Professor Flap said, "is learning how to control your movement. It's not just about speed—it's about balance and agility." Timmy listened carefully, eager to learn. He was a little nervous, but the thought of soaring through the air made his heart race with excitement. "Let's give it a try," Professor Flap said, flapping his wings and taking off into the sky. Timmy took a deep breath and followed.

At first, Timmy wobbled in the air, struggling to keep his balance. Flying was harder than it looked! But Professor Flap was patient, guiding him through each step. "Relax, Timmy. Feel the wind beneath you. Let it carry you," he said. Timmy closed his eyes and focused on the sensation of the wind. Slowly, he felt himself steady, and soon, he was flying smoothly through the air. "I'm doing it!" Timmy shouted, grinning from ear to ear. He flew higher, feeling the wind in his hair, the freedom of the open sky. It was better than he had ever imagined. "This is incredible!" he thought, soaring through the clouds.

Timmy's confidence grew with every flight. He practiced soaring over the floating platforms, zooming through obstacle courses, and even doing flips in the air. Each day, he got better and better, learning new tricks and improving his control. The more he flew, the more he felt like he truly belonged in Cartoon Land. Flying wasn't just his power—it was part of who he was. "You've come a long way," Professor Flap said one day after a particularly impressive flight. "You're becoming a real master of the skies." Timmy beamed with pride. He couldn't believe how much he had accomplished in such a short time.

One afternoon, after a long day of training, Timmy decided to take a solo flight around Cartoon Land. The sun was setting, casting a warm orange glow over the land, and Timmy couldn't resist the urge to explore. As he flew over the colorful buildings, he marveled at how different everything looked from above. He could see the entire town, the rivers, the mountains, and even the School of Superpowers in the distance. "This is amazing," Timmy thought as he soared through the sky, feeling completely free. He looped through the air, laughing with joy. Flying wasn't just a power—it was pure magic.

As Timmy continued his flight, he spotted Bingo waving from the ground. "Hey, Bingo!" Timmy called, swooping down to land next to his friend. "Look at you, Timmy! You're flying like a pro!" Bingo said, wagging his tail excitedly. Timmy grinned. "It's so much fun! I feel like I could fly forever." Bingo chuckled. "Well, you've certainly come a long way since your first day. You're a real superhero now!" Timmy's heart swelled with pride. He had discovered his superpower, made new friends, and was living the adventure of a lifetime. And the best part? This was just the beginning.

CHAPTER 4: THE MISCHIEF OF MR. SCRIBBLE

In the heart of Cartoon Land, there was one character everyone knew to be trouble—Mr. Scribble. He wasn't your typical cartoon villain; he was a wild, squiggly figure, constantly changing shape and size. His body was made of thick, wobbly lines, and he loved causing chaos wherever he went. Mr. Scribble had a mischievous grin that stretched across his face, and his eyes always glimmered with mischief. No one in Cartoon Land knew where he came from, but one thing was certain: wherever Mr. Scribble appeared, trouble followed. His latest scheme, however, was his most dastardly yet. Mr. Scribble had a plan to steal all the colors from Cartoon Land!

Mr. Scribble had always been jealous of the bright, beautiful colors that filled Cartoon Land. The greens of the trees, the blues of the sky, and the vibrant reds and yellows of the cartoon characters made the world feel alive. But Mr. Scribble, being made of black-and-white lines, didn't have any color of his own. "It's not fair!" he grumbled. "Why should they have all the colors while I'm stuck being boring and plain?" So, Mr. Scribble concocted a wicked plan. He would create a magic eraser powerful enough to suck up all the colors in Cartoon Land, leaving everything dull and lifeless. "Soon, everyone will be as colorless as me," he cackled.

One dark and stormy night, Mr. Scribble put his plan into action. With a flick of his wrist, he unleashed his magic eraser across Cartoon Land. At first, no one noticed anything unusual, but as the sun rose the next morning, something terrible happened. The bright, colorful world of Cartoon Land began to fade. The once-vibrant trees turned gray, the sky lost its blue hue, and the characters themselves started losing their colors. Flowers that once bloomed in rainbow shades now drooped in dull grays. Everywhere, the colors were disappearing, and Cartoon Land was turning into a black-and-white world. Panic spread like wildfire as everyone realized what was happening.

Timmy woke up that morning and couldn't believe his eyes. His bright red pajamas were now a sad, lifeless gray. The colorful posters on his walls had faded to dull tones, and even Bingo, who was usually a cheerful mix of brown and white, looked like he had been erased! "What's going on?!" Timmy exclaimed, rushing to the window. Outside, the world was losing its color faster than he could blink. "This has to be the work of Mr. Scribble!" Bingo barked, his ears drooping in concern. Timmy had heard of Mr. Scribble before, but he had never imagined the villain would do something this terrible. "We have to stop him!" Timmy declared.

But stopping Mr. Scribble wasn't going to be easy. "This is no ordinary villain," Bingo warned as they quickly got dressed and prepared to leave. "Mr. Scribble's magic eraser is incredibly powerful. If we don't stop him soon, all the colors in Cartoon Land will be gone forever!" Timmy's heart raced. The thought of living in a colorless world was too sad to bear. He loved the bright greens of the trees and the sunny yellows of the flowers. He couldn't let Mr. Scribble get away with this. "I don't care how hard it is," Timmy said with determination. "We have to find him and bring the colors back!"

With Bingo by his side, Timmy set off on the adventure of a lifetime. Armed with only their courage and the hope of saving Cartoon Land, they began their journey to track down Mr. Scribble. "Where do you think he could be hiding?" Timmy asked as they walked through the now colorless streets of Cartoon Town. Bingo scratched his head with his paw. "Knowing Mr. Scribble, he's probably somewhere dark and dreary—he loves gloomy places." Timmy nodded. That made sense. Mr. Scribble had always preferred shadows and storm clouds. But finding him was only half the battle. They would need to figure out how to reverse the erasing magic.

As they ventured deeper into Cartoon Land, the effects of Mr. Scribble's mischief became more apparent. The once-bustling streets were eerily quiet, and the usually cheerful cartoon characters were walking around with sad, gray faces. Even the animals in the forest seemed to have lost their joy. Birds that used to chirp in bright melodies now sang slow, mournful tunes. "This is awful," Timmy said, his heart heavy with sadness. "Cartoon Land was always so full of life. We can't let it stay like this." Bingo agreed, wagging his tail a little for encouragement. "Don't worry, Timmy. We'll stop Mr. Scribble. We just have to stay positive."

Their journey led them to the outskirts of Cartoon Land, where the sky was always gray, and the wind howled like a ghost. "This place gives me the creeps," Timmy said, shivering as they walked through the gloomy landscape. "It's just the kind of place Mr. Scribble would love," Bingo replied, his ears perking up as they followed a trail of squiggly lines that seemed to slither across the ground like snakes. Timmy knew they were getting closer. The squiggly lines were a sure sign that Mr. Scribble had been there recently. "We're on the right track," Timmy said, his heart pounding with a mix of fear and determination.

As they approached a dark, twisted cave, Timmy and Bingo stopped in their tracks. The entrance to the cave was guarded by two giant erasers, standing tall like sentinels. "This has to be it," Bingo whispered. Timmy swallowed hard. The cave looked ominous, but he knew they had no choice. "Ready, Bingo?" Timmy asked, his voice trembling just a little. "As ready as I'll ever be," Bingo replied, giving Timmy a brave nod. Together, they stepped forward, determined to face whatever challenges lay ahead. Inside the cave, the air was thick with darkness, and the walls seemed to ripple with Mr. Scribble's squiggly energy.

The deeper they ventured into the cave, the more the world seemed to change around them. The walls were covered in scribbles, lines twisting and curling like wild vines. It felt like they were walking into a maze made entirely of Mr. Scribble's chaotic energy. "Stay close," Timmy whispered to Bingo, his heart thudding in his chest. Bingo nodded, his nose twitching as he sniffed the air. The scent of eraser dust was everywhere. "We must be getting close to Mr. Scribble's lair," Bingo said, his voice barely audible over the eerie silence. Timmy clenched his fists. This was it—the final stretch.

Suddenly, they heard a raspy laugh echo through the cave. "Well, well, well, what do we have here?" Mr. Scribble's voice sneered. Timmy and Bingo froze. Out of the shadows, Mr. Scribble emerged, his squiggly body shifting and twisting with every step. "Did you really think you could stop me?" he taunted, waving his magic eraser in the air. "Cartoon Land will be gray forever, and there's nothing you can do about it!" Timmy's hands trembled, but he stood his ground. "We're here to bring the colors back, Mr. Scribble!" he shouted, his voice filled with courage. Bingo growled, ready to fight.

Mr. Scribble cackled, twirling the eraser in his hand. "You're too late! The colors are almost gone, and soon, they'll be erased forever!" he sneered, his eyes glinting with malice. Timmy's mind raced. How could they defeat Mr. Scribble? The magic eraser was too powerful to fight directly. But then, Timmy remembered something Professor Sparx had said at the School of Superpowers: "Every power, no matter how small, can make a difference." Timmy's eyes lit up. His power! Flying wouldn't help them defeat Mr. Scribble directly, but maybe it could help them in another way.

"Bingo, I have an idea!" Timmy whispered, leaning down to his friend. "I'll distract Mr. Scribble while you grab the eraser!" Bingo's eyes widened. "Are you sure?" Timmy nodded. "It's the only way. We have to stop him before it's too late!" With that, Timmy took off into the air, soaring around the cave in fast, dizzying circles. "Hey, Scribble Face! Bet you can't catch me!" he taunted, zooming past Mr. Scribble's head. Mr. Scribble snarled in frustration. "Stay still, you little pest!" he growled, swinging his eraser wildly. But Timmy was too quick. He darted around the cave, flying just out of reach.

While Mr. Scribble was distracted, Bingo made his move. Quietly, he crept up behind Mr. Scribble, his eyes locked on the magic eraser. "Almost there..." Bingo thought, inching closer. Finally, with a swift leap, Bingo snatched the eraser right out of Mr. Scribble's hand! "Got it!" he barked triumphantly. Mr. Scribble spun around in shock, his squiggly face twisting with rage. "No! Give that back!" he screamed, but it was too late. Bingo tossed the eraser to Timmy, who caught it in mid-air. "Let's see how you like being erased!" Timmy shouted, aiming the eraser at Mr. Scribble.

With a flash of light, the magic eraser unleashed its power—this time on Mr. Scribble himself! The villain's squiggly form began to dissolve, his lines unraveling like a piece of string. "Nooooooo!" Mr. Scribble howled as he faded away, leaving behind nothing but a puff of eraser dust. The cave fell silent, and for a moment, Timmy and Bingo just stared at each other, wide-eyed. "Did we... did we do it?" Timmy asked, his voice barely above a whisper. Bingo nodded, wagging his tail. "We did it, Timmy! We saved Cartoon Land!"

CHAPTER 5: JOURNEY TO THE DARK CAVE

Timmy and Bingo set off on their journey to find Mr. Scribble's hideout, navigating through the now colorless Cartoon Land. They traveled down a winding path that led them out of the familiar cartoon town and into the depths of a mysterious forest. The forest was unlike any they had seen before—it was a tangled mess of gnarled trees and thick underbrush, with shadows creeping across the ground like dark fingers. "This place feels spooky," Timmy said, glancing around nervously. The air was thick with an eerie silence, broken only by the rustling of leaves. Despite the unsettling atmosphere, Timmy knew they had to press on. "We have to find Mr. Scribble before it's too late," he said, trying to steady his trembling voice.

As they walked deeper into the forest, Timmy's fears began to grow. Every snap of a twig or rustle in the bushes made him jump, and the shadows seemed to dance and shift in the corners of his vision. "What if we never find the cave?" he wondered aloud. "What if Mr. Scribble is too powerful for us to defeat?" Doubts swirled in his mind, threatening to overwhelm him. The forest seemed endless, and the feeling of being watched made his skin crawl. "I don't know if I can do this," Timmy admitted, his voice shaking. He paused, feeling like the weight of the world was on his shoulders.

But Bingo, ever the loyal friend, was there to offer support. "Don't worry, Timmy," Bingo said, his tail wagging reassuringly. "We've come this far, and we're almost there. Remember, we're doing this to save Cartoon Land. You're braver than you think!" Bingo's words were like a warm hug in the cold, dark forest. Timmy took a deep breath, letting Bingo's encouragement wash over him. "You're right," he said, finding a bit of courage. "We can't give up now. We have to keep going, no matter how scary it gets."

Their journey wasn't without its challenges. The cartoon forest was filled with obstacles that seemed to come alive. They had to navigate through thorny bushes that reached out like grasping hands, and dodge low-hanging branches that tried to slap them in the face. At one point, they found themselves stuck in a muddy bog, with their feet sinking into the gooey ground. "We're stuck!" Timmy exclaimed, struggling to pull his feet free. "This is just one more thing to worry about." But Bingo, using his sharp instincts, found a narrow path around the bog. "This way!" he barked, leading Timmy to safer ground. Timmy followed, grateful for Bingo's guidance.

As they continued through the forest, they encountered a variety of new characters who offered their help. First, they met a wise old turtle named Tilly who was known for her knowledge of the forest's secrets. "You're headed for the Dark Cave, aren't you?" she asked, peering at them with her wise, old eyes. "Beware, for the path is fraught with danger. But fear not—I'll give you this enchanted lantern. It will light your way and reveal hidden paths." Tilly handed them a glowing lantern that shimmered with a soft, golden light. "Thank you, Tilly!" Timmy said, his spirits lifting. They continued on their journey, the lantern casting a comforting glow around them.

Next, they stumbled upon a cheerful group of fireflies who had been watching their progress. "We've heard you're on a dangerous mission," one firefly said, buzzing excitedly. "We'd be happy to guide you through the darkest parts of the forest. Follow us!" The fireflies flitted ahead, their tiny lights creating a trail through the darkness. Timmy and Bingo followed closely, feeling reassured by the friendly insects. "This is amazing!" Timmy said, watching as the forest transformed into a magical wonderland of twinkling lights. The fireflies led them to a hidden stream, where they could rest and refresh themselves before continuing.

The final stretch of their journey brought them to the entrance of the Dark Cave, where Mr. Scribble was hiding. The cave loomed ahead, its entrance dark and foreboding. "This is it," Timmy said, his heart pounding. The entrance to the cave was surrounded by tangled vines and thorns, and an ominous chill hung in the air. The cave seemed to swallow the light from their lantern, creating a deep, impenetrable darkness. Timmy took a deep breath, trying to steady his nerves. "We have to be brave," he told Bingo, who nodded in agreement. "We've come too far to turn back now."

As they entered the cave, the walls closed in around them, and the air grew colder. The tunnel was narrow and winding, with sharp rocks jutting out at odd angles. Timmy carefully navigated through the tight spaces, using the enchanted lantern to light their way. The cave echoed with the sounds of dripping water and distant whispers, adding to the eerie atmosphere. "I hope we're going the right way," Timmy said, his voice echoing off the cave walls. "We are," Bingo reassured him, sniffing the air for any sign of danger. "Mr. Scribble's hideout must be close."

Deeper and deeper they went, the darkness becoming almost tangible. The lantern's light flickered and danced on the cave walls, casting strange, shifting shadows. Timmy's mind raced with thoughts of what they might find ahead. Would Mr. Scribble be waiting for them? Would they be able to stop him before it was too late? "We can do this," Timmy whispered to himself, trying to push away his fear. "We have to do this." Bingo trotted beside him, his eyes alert and focused. Together, they pressed on, determined to find Mr. Scribble's lair.

At last, they reached a large, cavernous chamber at the heart of the cave. The chamber was vast and dark, with only the faintest glimmers of light coming from the flickering lantern. The air was thick with the smell of eraser dust and an uneasy silence. "This must be where Mr. Scribble is hiding," Timmy said, his voice barely more than a whisper. "We need to come up with a plan to confront him." Bingo looked around the chamber, his keen eyes searching for any sign of the villain. "Let's find a good vantage point and see if we can spot him," Bingo suggested. Timmy nodded, and they carefully moved to a higher ledge where they could get a better view.

As they surveyed the chamber from their vantage point, Timmy noticed a strange, swirling energy in the center of the room. It was the magic eraser that Mr. Scribble had used to steal the colors from Cartoon Land. The eraser was glowing ominously, and Timmy could see faint, twisted lines of black and white swirling around it. "That must be the source of his power," Timmy said, pointing to the eraser. "We have to find a way to stop it." Bingo agreed, his eyes fixed on the glowing eraser. "If we can destroy it or take it away from him, we might be able to reverse the damage he's done."

Timmy took a deep breath and began to formulate a plan. "We need to create a distraction to draw Mr. Scribble out of hiding," he said, thinking quickly. "Once he's distracted, we can grab the eraser and find a way to destroy it." Bingo nodded, understanding the plan. "I'll create a diversion by making some noise and drawing his attention," Bingo said. "While I do that, you'll have to be quick and find the eraser." Timmy nodded, feeling a surge of determination. "Let's do this," he said, steeling himself for the confrontation ahead.

With the plan in place, Bingo began to make noise, barking and howling to attract Mr. Scribble's attention. The sounds echoed through the chamber, bouncing off the walls and creating a cacophony of noise. Timmy watched as Mr. Scribble's squiggly form appeared from the shadows, his eyes glowing with anger. "What's all this racket?" Mr. Scribble snarled, looking around the chamber. As Mr. Scribble was distracted by the noise, Timmy seized the opportunity to slip down from the ledge and make his way toward the glowing magic eraser.

Timmy's heart pounded as he approached the eraser, trying to stay as quiet as possible. The eraser was pulsating with dark energy, and Timmy could feel its power radiating through the chamber. He reached out cautiously, his hands shaking as he grasped the eraser. Just as he was about to pull it away, Mr. Scribble turned and saw him. "Hey! What are you doing?" Mr. Scribble shouted, charging toward Timmy with an angry roar. Timmy's eyes widened in panic, but he held tight to the eraser, determined not to let it slip away.

As Mr. Scribble lunged at Timmy, Bingo leaped into action, barking loudly and causing a commotion. The distraction allowed Timmy to pull the eraser away from its pedestal and hold it up triumphantly. "We did it, Bingo!" Timmy shouted, feeling a rush of relief and triumph. "We've got the eraser!" Mr. Scribble's face twisted with rage as he realized his plan was falling apart. "No! You can't take it from me!" he howled, trying to snatch the eraser back. But with Bingo's help, Timmy was able to hold on and prepare for the final showdown.

CHAPTER 6: THE BATTLE FOR COLORS

Timmy and Bingo stood at the entrance of the Dark Cave, their hearts racing as they prepared to face Mr. Scribble. The cave's ominous entrance seemed to swallow the light from their lantern, creating a deep, impenetrable darkness. "This is it," Timmy said, his voice trembling slightly. "We need to be careful and stay focused." With a deep breath, they stepped into the cave, their footsteps echoing off the stone walls. The air grew colder and the shadows seemed to grow longer as they ventured deeper. Timmy's mind raced with thoughts of what awaited them inside, but he knew they had to press on.

As they progressed through the winding tunnels, they suddenly encountered Mr. Scribble's shadowy guards. These guards were eerie, dark shapes that seemed to flicker in and out of existence, their forms constantly shifting and morphing. "Halt!" one of the guards growled, extending a shadowy arm to block their path. Timmy and Bingo braced themselves as the guards advanced, their menacing eyes glowing with a dark energy. "We're not stopping!" Timmy shouted, his voice filled with determination. With a burst of energy, Bingo leaped forward, distracting the guards with a series of sharp barks. Timmy used this opportunity to dart past them, hoping to reach Mr. Scribble's lair before it was too late.

The deeper they went, the more intense the atmosphere became. Soon, Timmy and Bingo reached the heart of the cave, where Mr. Scribble was waiting for them. The villain's squiggly form was more menacing than ever, his eyes blazing with fury. "You're too late!" Mr. Scribble sneered, his voice echoing off the cave walls. "The colors are mine to control!" Timmy felt a surge of fear but quickly pushed it aside. "Not if we can help it!" he shouted back, stepping forward to confront the villain. The tension in the air was palpable as the battle began.

The battle between Timmy and Mr. Scribble was fierce and chaotic. Mr. Scribble hurled dark, twisting lines at Timmy, who narrowly avoided them by using his flying abilities. "You'll never defeat me!" Mr. Scribble roared, sending a wave of shadowy energy toward Timmy. Timmy soared through the air, dodging the attacks and using his speed to his advantage. With each pass, Timmy looked for an opening, trying to find a way to gain the upper hand. Bingo circled around, barking and trying to distract Mr. Scribble from above. The fight seemed endless, but Timmy's resolve only grew stronger.

Timmy's flying skills proved to be a crucial advantage in the battle. He darted and weaved through the air, outmaneuvering Mr. Scribble's attacks with ease. "You're not so tough when you can't hit your target!" Timmy taunted, using his speed to his advantage. Mr. Scribble's frustration grew with each failed attack, his shadowy form flickering with rage. Timmy took advantage of Mr. Scribble's anger, performing daring aerial maneuvers to stay one step ahead. "I need to find a way to end this!" Timmy thought, scanning the cave for anything that could help him in the fight. His eyes fell on a faint, colorful glow coming from the corner of the cavern.

Timmy's attention was drawn to a shimmering light hidden in the depths of the cave. As he approached, he discovered the rainbow crystal, its radiant colors pulsating with a magical energy. "That's it!" Timmy realized, recognizing the crystal as the source of the colors stolen from Cartoon Land. "If I can get that crystal back, we might be able to restore everything!" With renewed determination, Timmy swooped down toward the crystal, carefully avoiding Mr. Scribble's attacks. The crystal was encased in a protective field of shadowy energy, making it difficult to reach. "I have to find a way through," Timmy thought, focusing on the task at hand.

Seeing the crystal made Timmy more determined than ever to stop Mr. Scribble. With a surge of bravery, Timmy made a daring move to reclaim the crystal. He flew directly at the protective field, using his agility to dodge the swirling shadows. "I'm not giving up!" Timmy shouted as he reached for the crystal. His fingers brushed against its smooth surface, and a burst of color exploded from the crystal, illuminating the cave with a brilliant light. The protective field shattered, and Timmy grabbed the crystal, holding it aloft with triumph. "We did it, Bingo!" Timmy cheered, feeling a wave of relief and victory.

With the rainbow crystal in hand, Timmy and Bingo prepared to leave the cave and restore the colors to Cartoon Land. But Mr. Scribble wasn't finished yet. "You can't take it from me!" he bellowed, trying to snatch the crystal back. Timmy and Bingo dashed toward the exit, narrowly avoiding Mr. Scribble's desperate attacks. The cave's entrance grew closer, and Timmy could see the light from outside. "Almost there!" Timmy urged, pushing himself to fly faster. Bingo barked encouragement, his eyes fixed on the glowing exit ahead.

As they emerged from the cave, the light of Cartoon Land flooded over them, casting away the shadows of the Dark Cave. Timmy and Bingo raced toward the town, eager to restore the colors that had been stolen. "Hold on, Cartoon Land!" Timmy shouted, clutching the rainbow crystal tightly. The crystal began to glow brightly, its colors swirling and mixing in a dazzling display. "This is it!" Timmy said, feeling a rush of excitement. He could see the once-colorless town beginning to brighten up, the hues returning to their vibrant glory.

The colors began to spread throughout Cartoon Land, revitalizing everything they touched. Trees turned from gray to green, flowers bloomed in brilliant shades, and buildings regained their cheerful, lively colors. "It's working!" Timmy exclaimed, watching in awe as the town transformed before his eyes. The citizens of Cartoon Land emerged from their homes, their faces lighting up with joy as they saw the vibrant world around them. "Thank you, Timmy!" they cheered, their voices filled with gratitude. Timmy and Bingo stood proudly as the colors of Cartoon Land were fully restored.

With the return of the colors, the joy and energy of Cartoon Land were palpable. Timmy and Bingo were greeted with cheers and celebrations as they made their way through the town. "We couldn't have done it without you," one of the townsfolk said, shaking Timmy's hand. "You saved our world!" Timmy smiled, feeling a deep sense of accomplishment. "It was a team effort," he said, looking at Bingo with a grin. "We couldn't have done it without each other."

Mr. Scribble's dark influence was gone, and the cave was now a place of light and color, thanks to Timmy and Bingo's bravery. The once-menacing villain was nowhere to be seen, his plans thwarted by the power of teamwork and courage. "We really did it," Timmy said, taking in the colorful, vibrant world around him. "Cartoon Land is safe once again." Bingo wagged his tail happily, his eyes shining with pride. "We made a great team," he said, nuzzling Timmy affectionately.

As the sun set over Cartoon Land, casting a warm, golden glow over the town, Timmy and Bingo celebrated their victory with their new friends. They were honored with a grand feast, filled with delicious foods and lively music. "This has been an adventure I'll never forget," Timmy said, looking around at the joyful faces of Cartoon Land's residents. "Thank you all for your support and friendship." The townsfolk cheered, lifting Timmy and Bingo onto their shoulders in celebration. "To Timmy and Bingo, our heroes!" they shouted.

The celebration continued late into the night, with laughter and dancing filling the air. Timmy felt a deep sense of satisfaction, knowing that he had made a difference in this magical world. "I'm glad we could help," Timmy said to Bingo, as they watched the stars twinkle above. "It was an amazing adventure." Bingo barked in agreement, his tail wagging in delight. "We did good, Timmy," he said. "And we'll always have these memories to treasure."

As the festivities wound down and the night grew quiet, Timmy and Bingo found a peaceful spot to rest. They lay on a grassy hill, gazing up at the night sky, which was now filled with vibrant colors from the restored rainbow crystal. "This is beautiful," Timmy said, his voice filled with wonder. "It's like a dream." Bingo snuggled close, his eyes drooping with exhaustion. "We've earned this rest," he said, closing his eyes. "Tomorrow is a new day, and we'll be ready for whatever comes next."

The adventure had come to a close, but Timmy knew that the memories of their journey would stay with him forever. He and Bingo had faced challenges, made new friends, and restored the colors to Cartoon Land. "What an amazing adventure we've had," Timmy said, smiling as he drifted off to sleep. "Thank you for being with me through it all." Bingo sighed contentedly, his dreams filled with the vibrant colors of Cartoon Land. Together, they dreamed of the endless possibilities that awaited them in the future, knowing that they could face anything as long as they were together.

As the colors continued to spread throughout Cartoon Land, Timmy and Bingo took a moment to catch their breath and reflect on their journey. The once bleak and colorless landscape had transformed into a vibrant, lively world full of joy and energy. "It's incredible," Timmy said, looking around at the restored beauty of the town. "I never imagined it would look like this again." Bingo's eyes sparkled with happiness as he saw the smiling faces of their friends and neighbors. "We did something amazing today," Bingo said, wagging his tail. "It's like magic!"

Timmy and Bingo decided to take a leisurely stroll through the town to see the full extent of the changes. They wandered past colorful houses, blooming gardens, and bustling streets filled with cheerful residents. "Look at that!" Timmy pointed out as he saw a giant mural painted on a wall, depicting the history of Cartoon Land in vibrant colors. The mural showed Timmy and Bingo at the center, their heroic deeds immortalized in paint. "We're part of the story now," Timmy said, feeling a sense of pride. Bingo barked happily, his eyes filled with admiration.

As they continued their walk, Timmy and Bingo were approached by the mayor of Cartoon Land, a friendly character named Mayor Jolly.

"Timmy, Bingo, you've done an incredible job!" Mayor Jolly exclaimed, his voice filled with gratitude. "We're forever grateful for your bravery and determination." He handed them a beautifully crafted medal, adorned with colorful gems. "This is for you, as a token of our appreciation," Mayor Jolly said, placing the medal around Timmy's neck. Timmy smiled, touched by the gesture. "Thank you, Mayor Jolly," he said. "It means a lot to us."

The celebration in Cartoon Land continued with a grand parade, where Timmy and Bingo were the guests of honor. The streets were lined with excited residents, all cheering and waving as the parade made its way through town. "This is amazing!" Timmy said, feeling overwhelmed by the attention. Bingo barked in excitement, enjoying the festive atmosphere. Floats decorated with colorful flowers and balloons passed by, and music filled the air. Timmy and Bingo waved and smiled, feeling a deep sense of joy and accomplishment.

As the parade drew to a close, Timmy and Bingo were invited to a special ceremony in the town square. The citizens gathered around, eager to hear Timmy's thoughts on their adventure. "It's been an incredible journey," Timmy began, addressing the crowd. "We've faced challenges and overcome obstacles, but we did it together. The real hero is every one of you who stood by us and helped along the way." The crowd erupted into cheers, applauding Timmy and Bingo's bravery and teamwork.

Later that evening, as the town settled down and the festivities came to an end, Timmy and Bingo took a quiet walk to the edge of town. They sat on a hill overlooking Cartoon Land, watching as the sun set in a spectacular display of colors. "It's beautiful," Timmy said, feeling a deep sense of contentment. "I'll never forget this day." Bingo lay beside him, his head resting on Timmy's lap. "We've had an incredible adventure," Bingo said softly. "And now we get to enjoy the world we saved."

As they sat together, Timmy thought about all the friends they had made and the lessons they had learned. He realized that the true magic of Cartoon Land wasn't just in its colors, but in the friendships and experiences they had shared. "I'm grateful for this adventure," Timmy said, looking at Bingo. "It's taught me so much about bravery and friendship." Bingo nuzzled Timmy affectionately, his eyes reflecting the colors of the sunset. "We make a great team," he said. "And we'll always have these memories."

The following morning, Timmy and Bingo prepared to say their goodbyes to Cartoon Land. "It's time for us to return home," Timmy said, feeling a mix of excitement and sadness. "But we'll always carry these memories with us." The residents of Cartoon Land gathered to bid them farewell, their faces filled with smiles and gratitude. "Thank you for everything," Mayor Jolly said, shaking Timmy's hand. "You're always welcome here." Timmy and Bingo hugged their friends, feeling a deep sense of connection. "We'll miss you all," Timmy said, his voice filled with emotion.

As Timmy and Bingo stepped through the portal back to their world, they looked back one last time at Cartoon Land, their hearts full of fond memories. "Goodbye, Cartoon Land," Timmy whispered. "Thank you for the adventure." The portal closed behind them, and they found themselves back in their own world, the familiar sights and sounds of their home surrounding them. "We made it!" Timmy said, grinning at Bingo. "What an adventure!"

Bingo wagged his tail, looking up at Timmy with a happy expression. "We sure did," he said. "And who knows what other adventures await us in the future?" Timmy nodded, feeling a sense of excitement for what lies ahead. "I can't wait to see what comes next," Timmy said, his eyes sparkling with anticipation. As they walked home, Timmy and Bingo knew that they had not only saved Cartoon Land but had also discovered the true magic of friendship and adventure.

CHAPTER 7: CELEBRATION IN CARTOON LAND

The colors were back, and Cartoon Land had transformed into a spectacular feast for the eyes. Timmy watched in awe as vibrant hues spread across the landscape, painting the sky in brilliant shades of pink, blue, and gold. The once-gray trees and buildings now shimmered with renewed life, their colors dancing in the sunlight. Everywhere Timmy looked, the world seemed to burst with energy and joy. Flowers bloomed in an explosion of color, and the streets were filled with excited chatter. The people of Cartoon Land emerged from their homes, their faces alight with happiness as they took in the beauty around them. It was clear that the return of the colors meant more to them than just visual splendor; it was a sign of hope and renewal.

The citizens of Cartoon Land gathered in the town square, their faces brimming with gratitude and excitement. "Timmy! Bingo!" they cheered as Timmy and his loyal companion entered the square, their arrival greeted with enthusiastic applause. "You've saved our world!" one character exclaimed, waving a colorful flag. Balloons floated above the crowd, and confetti rained down in a joyous display. The townsfolk gathered around Timmy and Bingo, showering them with praise and admiration. "We couldn't have done it without you," Mayor Jolly said, extending a hand in thanks. Timmy felt a rush of pride as he looked around at the smiling faces of his new friends.

As the festivities continued, Timmy's mind began to reflect on what it meant to be a true hero. He realized that heroism wasn't just about performing grand acts of bravery; it was about the courage to face challenges and the strength to persevere. Timmy thought about the support he received from Bingo and the friends he made along the way. "Being a hero isn't about doing it alone," Timmy mused, "it's about working together and believing in each other." He felt a deep sense of fulfillment, knowing that his actions had made a real difference. The joy of the celebration was matched only by the warmth he felt in his heart.

The lessons Timmy had learned from his adventure became clear as he looked around at the lively celebrations. He had discovered the power of friendship, the importance of perseverance, and the value of teamwork. The experience had taught him that true strength came from within and that even the smallest acts of bravery could lead to significant change. Timmy realized that these lessons were as valuable as the victory itself. "It's not just about saving the day," Timmy thought, "it's about growing and learning along the way." He felt grateful for the journey and the wisdom it had brought him.

The celebration reached its peak with a grand party thrown in Timmy's honor. The streets were lined with colorful decorations, and a large stage was set up for performances. Music filled the air, and people danced joyfully, their movements a blur of color and energy. Tables groaned under the weight of delicious foods, from vibrant fruit platters to elaborate cakes. Timmy and Bingo mingled with their new friends, sharing stories and laughter. "This is amazing!" Timmy exclaimed, his eyes wide with delight. The party was a fitting tribute to their adventure, and Timmy felt overwhelmed by the outpouring of love and appreciation.

As the evening wore on, Timmy was called to the center of the square for a special recognition ceremony. Mayor Jolly stood beside him, holding a beautifully crafted trophy that glowed with a magical light. "Timmy, you have shown incredible bravery and selflessness," Mayor Jolly announced, holding up the trophy for everyone to see. "This trophy is a symbol of our gratitude and admiration." The crowd erupted into cheers as Timmy accepted the trophy, his face flushed with pride. "Thank you, everyone," Timmy said, his voice filled with emotion. "I couldn't have done it without all of you."

The bond between Timmy and Bingo grew stronger as they celebrated their victory. They shared a quiet moment together, watching the festivities from a cozy spot on a hill. "We did it, Bingo," Timmy said, resting a hand on his friend's head. Bingo nuzzled Timmy affectionately, his eyes sparkling with happiness. "We sure did," Bingo replied, his voice warm and reassuring. The adventure had brought them even closer, and they both knew that their friendship was the real treasure of their journey. As they looked out over the joyous scene, they felt a deep sense of contentment and unity.

The celebration continued late into the night, with fireworks lighting up the sky in a dazzling display. The colors of the fireworks mirrored the vibrant hues of Cartoon Land, creating a magical spectacle that left everyone in awe. Timmy and Bingo watched in wonder as the sky erupted in bursts of red, green, and blue. "This is the best ending to an adventure I could have imagined," Timmy said, his eyes reflecting the brilliant lights. Bingo barked in agreement, his tail wagging with excitement. The night sky was a fitting canvas for their triumphant return, and Timmy felt a profound sense of joy and accomplishment.

As the party drew to a close, Timmy and Bingo took a moment to thank their new friends for the unforgettable experience. "We couldn't have asked for a better celebration," Timmy said, shaking hands with Mayor Jolly and other key figures. The mayor smiled warmly, his eyes twinkling with gratitude. "You're always welcome here," Mayor Jolly said, extending an invitation for future visits. Timmy and Bingo felt a deep sense of belonging and were touched by the generous offer. "We'll definitely come back to visit," Timmy promised, feeling a pang of sadness as the time to leave approached.

The next morning, Timmy and Bingo prepared for their departure, saying their goodbyes to the friends they had made. The residents of Cartoon Land gathered to bid them farewell, their faces a mixture of sadness and gratitude. "We'll miss you," one of the characters said, holding back tears. "You've been such a wonderful part of our world." Timmy hugged each of his friends, feeling a sense of warmth and connection. "I'll miss you all too," Timmy said, his voice choked with emotion. "Thank you for everything."

As they walked toward the portal that would take them back home, Timmy and Bingo looked back one last time at the colorful, vibrant world they had helped save. "Goodbye, Cartoon Land," Timmy whispered, feeling a mixture of excitement and sadness. The portal shimmered with a magical light, beckoning them back to their own world. "It's time to go," Bingo said, his voice filled with a sense of anticipation. Timmy nodded, taking one final look at the place that had become so dear to them.

The portal closed behind them, and they found themselves back in their familiar world, the sights and sounds of home surrounding them. "We made it!" Timmy exclaimed, his heart racing with excitement. "What an adventure!" Bingo looked around, his eyes filled with wonder. "I can't wait to tell everyone about our adventure," he said, wagging his tail. Timmy smiled, knowing that their experiences in Cartoon Land would be cherished memories forever.

As they walked home, Timmy and Bingo talked about their favorite moments from the adventure. "Remember the parade?" Timmy said, his eyes sparkling with excitement. "That was incredible!" Bingo nodded in agreement, his tail wagging enthusiastically. "And the fireworks!" Bingo added. "That was the perfect ending to our adventure." Timmy felt a deep sense of satisfaction, knowing that their journey had been an unforgettable experience.

Back at home, Timmy and Bingo settled into their routine, but their adventure in Cartoon Land remained a cherished memory. They often reminisced about their time in the magical world and the friends they had made. "We really did something special," Timmy said, looking at Bingo with a smile. Bingo nuzzled Timmy affectionately, his eyes filled with happiness. "We sure did," he said. "And we'll always have these memories to treasure."

Timmy's adventure had taught him valuable lessons about bravery, friendship, and the power of teamwork. He carried these lessons with him as he went about his daily life, feeling more confident and inspired. "I'm grateful for everything we experienced," Timmy said, looking at the world around him with new eyes. Bingo agreed, his tail wagging in contentment. "We've learned so much and made so many wonderful memories," Bingo said.

The experience in Cartoon Land had not only been an adventure but had also brought Timmy and Bingo closer together. Their bond was stronger than ever, and they knew that they could face any challenge as long as they had each other. "We make a great team," Timmy said, patting Bingo on the head. Bingo barked happily, his eyes shining with affection. "We sure do," he agreed. "And I can't wait to see what adventures lie ahead."

As the days passed, Timmy and Bingo continued to enjoy their everyday lives, but they never forgot the magical world of Cartoon Land. They looked forward to their next adventure, knowing that the lessons they had learned and the friendships they had made would always be a part of them. "We've had an incredible journey," Timmy said, his eyes sparkling with anticipation. "And there's always more to explore." Bingo wagged his tail, eager for whatever came next. "I'm ready for the next adventure," he said, his voice filled with excitement.

Their adventure in Cartoon Land had been a journey of discovery and growth, filled with unforgettable moments and cherished memories. Timmy and Bingo knew that the magic of their adventure would stay with them forever. "Thank you for being part of this adventure," Timmy said, looking at Bingo with a grateful smile.

CHAPTER 8: MORE ADVENTURES AWAIT

Timmy's curiosity was piqued as he gazed out over Cartoon Land, eager to explore more of the magical world he had recently saved. "There's so much more to discover," Timmy said, his eyes sparkling with excitement. He thought about the colorful places he had already visited and wondered what other wonders awaited them. The vibrant landscapes and charming characters had left him wanting to see every corner of this enchanting world. "I wonder what else Cartoon Land has to offer," Timmy mused aloud. Bingo, who had been enjoying a nap beside him, perked up at the mention of more adventures. "There are plenty of amazing places we haven't seen yet," Bingo said, his tail wagging eagerly.

Bingo suggested a few places that Timmy might find interesting. "How about visiting the Candy Mountains?" Bingo proposed with a mischievous grin. "They're made entirely of candy, and the view from the top is incredible." Timmy's eyes widened at the thought of mountains made of sweets. "That sounds like a dream come true," Timmy said, imagining himself climbing giant chocolate peaks and sliding down sugary slopes. "And we could also explore the Magical Forest," Bingo continued. "It's a place full of wonder and mystery, with trees that can talk and flowers that sing."

The two friends set off for the Candy Mountains, their excitement growing with each step. As they approached, Timmy could hardly believe his eyes; the mountains glistened in the sunlight like giant, colorful candy canes. "Wow, this is even more amazing than I imagined!" Timmy exclaimed, his face lit up with awe. They climbed up the candy-coated slopes, tasting the sweet treats as they went. "This chocolate is delicious!" Timmy said, savoring a piece of the mountain. Bingo happily nibbled on a candy cane, his eyes shining with joy. "I told you it would be fun," Bingo said, wagging his tail in delight.

Next, they ventured into the Magical Forest, where the trees were tall and twisted, their leaves shimmering in a spectrum of colors. "This place is like something out of a fairy tale," Timmy said, gazing around in wonder. The forest was alive with magical creatures, from sparkling fireflies to singing flowers. "Hello there!" one of the flowers chimed as they passed by. Timmy and Bingo greeted the friendly flora with smiles and waves. They wandered deeper into the forest, marveling at the talking trees and the gentle, magical creatures that fluttered around them. "This is incredible," Timmy said, feeling like he had stepped into another world.

During their adventures, Timmy and Bingo met new friends with unique powers, each one adding to the richness of Cartoon Land. "This is Twinkle," a sparkling fairy introduced herself, flitting gracefully around them. "She has the ability to make things glow with her magical light." Twinkle showed them how her light could create beautiful patterns in the air. "And this is Fluffernut," a fluffy creature with the power to create gentle breezes. Fluffernut demonstrated his power by making a cool breeze swirl around them. "It's amazing how many different powers everyone has here," Timmy said, feeling inspired by the diversity of abilities.

Timmy's confidence in his own abilities grew as he spent more time exploring Cartoon Land. He practiced his flying skills, soaring higher and faster with each attempt. "Look at me, Bingo!" Timmy shouted, performing a loop-de-loop in the sky. "You're doing great!" Bingo cheered from below, his eyes following Timmy's every move. Timmy felt a sense of accomplishment as he mastered new flying techniques, knowing that his adventure had made him stronger and more capable. "I'm really starting to get the hang of this," Timmy said, feeling proud of his progress.

As they continued their journey, Timmy and Bingo took on small problems around Cartoon Land, using their skills and teamwork to help those in need. They fixed broken bridges, helped lost animals find their way home, and repaired magical fountains that had gone dry. "It feels good to help out," Timmy said, smiling as he worked alongside Bingo. The residents of Cartoon Land were grateful for their assistance, showering them with thanks and praise. "You're always welcome to help us," one character said, offering Timmy and Bingo a basket of treats. "It's the least we can do to show our appreciation."

One day, as they were enjoying a peaceful afternoon, Timmy and Bingo noticed something strange in the distance. A thick fog had rolled in, and it seemed to be swirling around a particular area of Cartoon Land. "That looks suspicious," Timmy said, narrowing his eyes. "I wonder what's going on over there." Bingo's ears perked up with curiosity. "Let's check it out," he suggested. The two friends decided to investigate, eager to uncover the source of the mysterious fog.

As they approached the foggy area, they saw that the fog was emanating from a hidden cave. "I've never seen this cave before," Timmy said, peering into the darkness. "It looks like it's been concealed by the fog." Bingo nodded in agreement, his nose twitching as he sniffed the air. "It could be hiding something important," Bingo said, his voice filled with determination. Timmy and Bingo steeled themselves for another adventure, knowing that they would need to be brave and resourceful to uncover the mystery.

The entrance to the cave was narrow and dark, but Timmy and Bingo pressed on, their excitement outweighing their apprehension. "We'll need to be careful," Timmy said, taking a deep breath as they stepped inside. The cave was filled with glittering crystals and strange markings on the walls. "This place is amazing," Timmy said, his eyes wide with wonder. "It's like stepping into a hidden world." Bingo sniffed the air, alert for any signs of danger. "Let's see what secrets this cave holds," Bingo said, his voice filled with anticipation.

As they ventured deeper into the cave, they encountered a series of challenges that tested their skills and courage. They navigated through narrow passages, solved riddles, and avoided hidden traps. "This is definitely going to be a challenge," Timmy said, sweating from the effort. "But we've faced challenges before." Bingo nodded, his determination unwavering. "We can do this," Bingo said, his eyes shining with resolve. Together, they worked through each obstacle, their teamwork and ingenuity guiding them toward their goal.

Eventually, they reached the heart of the cave, where they discovered an ancient artifact glowing with a soft, magical light. "This must be what the fog was hiding," Timmy said, his eyes widening in awe. The artifact was a beautifully crafted amulet, adorned with intricate patterns and sparkling gemstones. "It looks incredibly important," Bingo said, examining the amulet closely. Timmy carefully picked up the amulet, feeling a sense of awe and reverence. "I wonder what this amulet does," Timmy said, holding it up to the light.

As Timmy and Bingo prepared to leave the cave with their new discovery, they noticed a hidden compartment in the wall. Inside, they found an old journal filled with notes and drawings about the amulet. "This journal could hold important information," Timmy said, flipping through the pages. The notes revealed that the amulet had the power to enhance the abilities of those who possessed it. "This could be a valuable tool for our future adventures," Bingo said, his eyes gleaming with excitement. Timmy and Bingo carefully packed up the journal and amulet, eager to learn more about their newfound treasure.

As they made their way back to Cartoon Land, Timmy and Bingo felt a renewed sense of excitement for the adventures that lay ahead. "We've uncovered a great mystery," Timmy said, his voice filled with anticipation. "And who knows what other secrets Cartoon Land holds." Bingo agreed, his tail wagging happily. "I'm ready for whatever comes next," Bingo said, his eyes sparkling with enthusiasm. Timmy and Bingo knew that their journey was far from over and that more adventures awaited them in the magical world they had come to love.

Back in Cartoon Land, they were greeted by their friends, who were eager to hear about their latest adventure. Timmy and Bingo shared their discovery with excitement, showing off the amulet and journal. "This is incredible!" one of their friends said, marveling at the artifact. "You two are always finding amazing things." Timmy and Bingo smiled, feeling proud of their latest achievement. "We couldn't have done it without your support," Timmy said, grateful for the encouragement of his friends.

As they settled into their routine, Timmy and Bingo continued to explore Cartoon Land, always on the lookout for new adventures. The amulet and journal became valuable tools in their quest to uncover the secrets of their magical world. "I'm looking forward to seeing what else we can discover," Timmy said, his eyes filled with excitement. Bingo agreed, his tail wagging eagerly. "Here's to many more adventures," Bingo said, his voice brimming with enthusiasm. Timmy and Bingo knew that their journey was just beginning and that the future held countless possibilities for exploration and discovery.

The adventures in Cartoon Land had shown Timmy and Bingo the magic of exploration and the joy of uncovering new mysteries. They embraced each day with a sense of wonder and curiosity, eager to see what lay beyond the horizon. "Every day is a new adventure," Timmy said, looking out over the colorful world he had come to love. Bingo nodded in agreement, his eyes shining with excitement. "And I wouldn't have it any other way," Bingo said, his voice filled with happiness. Timmy and Bingo knew that their adventures would continue, and they looked forward to every new challenge and discovery with open hearts and eager spirits.

CHAPTER 9: TIME TO GO HOME

Timmy's curiosity was piqued as he gazed out over Cartoon Land, eager to explore more of the magical world he had recently saved. "There's so much more to discover," Timmy said, his eyes sparkling with excitement. He thought about the colorful places he had already visited and wondered what other wonders awaited them. The vibrant landscapes and charming characters had left him wanting to see every corner of this enchanting world. "I wonder what else Cartoon Land has to offer," Timmy mused aloud. Bingo, who had been enjoying a nap beside him, perked up at the mention of more adventures. "There are plenty of amazing places we haven't seen yet," Bingo said, his tail wagging eagerly.

Bingo suggested a few places that Timmy might find interesting. "How about visiting the Candy Mountains?" Bingo proposed with a mischievous grin. "They're made entirely of candy, and the view from the top is incredible." Timmy's eyes widened at the thought of mountains made of sweets. "That sounds like a dream come true," Timmy said, imagining himself climbing giant chocolate peaks and sliding down sugary slopes. "And we could also explore the Magical Forest," Bingo continued. "It's a place full of wonder and mystery, with trees that can talk and flowers that sing."

The two friends set off for the Candy Mountains, their excitement growing with each step. As they approached, Timmy could hardly believe his eyes; the mountains glistened in the sunlight like giant, colorful candy canes. "Wow, this is even more amazing than I imagined!" Timmy exclaimed, his face lit up with awe. They climbed up the candy-coated slopes, tasting the sweet treats as they went. "This chocolate is delicious!" Timmy said, savoring a piece of the mountain. Bingo happily nibbled on a candy cane, his eyes shining with joy. "I told you it would be fun," Bingo said, wagging his tail in delight.

Next, they ventured into the Magical Forest, where the trees were tall and twisted, their leaves shimmering in a spectrum of colors. "This place is like something out of a fairy tale," Timmy said, gazing around in wonder. The forest was alive with magical creatures, from sparkling fireflies to singing flowers. "Hello there!" one of the flowers chimed as they passed by. Timmy and Bingo greeted the friendly flora with smiles and waves. They wandered deeper into the forest, marveling at the talking trees and the gentle, magical creatures that fluttered around them. "This is incredible," Timmy said, feeling like he had stepped into another world.

During their adventures, Timmy and Bingo met new friends with unique powers, each one adding to the richness of Cartoon Land. "This is Twinkle," a sparkling fairy introduced herself, flitting gracefully around them. "She has the ability to make things glow with her magical light." Twinkle showed them how her light could create beautiful patterns in the air. "And this is Fluffernut," a fluffy creature with the power to create gentle breezes. Fluffernut demonstrated his power by making a cool breeze swirl around them. "It's amazing how many different powers everyone has here," Timmy said, feeling inspired by the diversity of abilities.

Timmy's confidence in his own abilities grew as he spent more time exploring Cartoon Land. He practiced his flying skills, soaring higher and faster with each attempt. "Look at me, Bingo!" Timmy shouted, performing a loop-de-loop in the sky. "You're doing great!" Bingo cheered from below, his eyes following Timmy's every move. Timmy felt a sense of accomplishment as he mastered new flying techniques, knowing that his adventure had made him stronger and more capable. "I'm really starting to get the hang of this," Timmy said, feeling proud of his progress.

As they continued their journey, Timmy and Bingo took on small problems around Cartoon Land, using their skills and teamwork to help those in need. They fixed broken bridges, helped lost animals find their way home, and repaired magical fountains that had gone dry. "It feels good to help out," Timmy said, smiling as he worked alongside Bingo.

The residents of Cartoon Land were grateful for their assistance, showering them with thanks and praise. "You're always welcome to help us," one character said, offering Timmy and Bingo a basket of treats. "It's the least we can do to show our appreciation."

One day, as they were enjoying a peaceful afternoon, Timmy and Bingo noticed something strange in the distance. A thick fog had rolled in, and it seemed to be swirling around a particular area of Cartoon Land. "That looks suspicious," Timmy said, narrowing his eyes. "I wonder what's going on over there." Bingo's ears perked up with curiosity. "Let's check it out," he suggested. The two friends decided to investigate, eager to uncover the source of the mysterious fog.

As they approached the foggy area, they saw that the fog was emanating from a hidden cave. "I've never seen this cave before," Timmy said, peering into the darkness. "It looks like it's been concealed by the fog." Bingo nodded in agreement, his nose twitching as he sniffed the air. "It could be hiding something important," Bingo said, his voice filled with determination. Timmy and Bingo steeled themselves for another adventure, knowing that they would need to be brave and resourceful to uncover the mystery.

The entrance to the cave was narrow and dark, but Timmy and Bingo pressed on, their excitement outweighing their apprehension. "We'll need to be careful," Timmy said, taking a deep breath as they stepped inside. The cave was filled with glittering crystals and strange markings on the walls. "This place is amazing," Timmy said, his eyes wide with wonder. "It's like stepping into a hidden world." Bingo sniffed the air, alert for any signs of danger. "Let's see what secrets this cave holds," Bingo said, his voice filled with anticipation.

As they ventured deeper into the cave, they encountered a series of challenges that tested their skills and courage. They navigated through narrow passages, solved riddles, and avoided hidden traps. "This is definitely going to be a challenge," Timmy said, sweating from the effort. "But we've faced challenges before." Bingo nodded, his determination unwavering. "We can do this," Bingo said, his eyes shining with resolve. Together, they worked through each obstacle, their teamwork and ingenuity guiding them toward their goal.

Eventually, they reached the heart of the cave, where they discovered an ancient artifact glowing with a soft, magical light. "This must be what the fog was hiding," Timmy said, his eyes widening in awe. The artifact was a beautifully crafted amulet, adorned with intricate patterns and sparkling gemstones. "It looks incredibly important," Bingo said, examining the amulet closely. Timmy carefully picked up the amulet, feeling a sense of awe and reverence. "I wonder what this amulet does," Timmy said, holding it up to the light.

As Timmy and Bingo prepared to leave the cave with their new discovery, they noticed a hidden compartment in the wall. Inside, they found an old journal filled with notes and drawings about the amulet. "This journal could hold important information," Timmy said, flipping through the pages. The notes revealed that the amulet had the power to enhance the abilities of those who possessed it. "This could be a valuable tool for our future adventures," Bingo said, his eyes gleaming with excitement. Timmy and Bingo carefully packed up the journal and amulet, eager to learn more about their newfound treasure.

As they made their way back to Cartoon Land, Timmy and Bingo felt a renewed sense of excitement for the adventures that lay ahead. "We've uncovered a great mystery," Timmy said, his voice filled with anticipation. "And who knows what other secrets Cartoon Land holds." Bingo agreed, his tail wagging happily. "I'm ready for whatever comes next," Bingo said, his eyes sparkling with enthusiasm. Timmy and Bingo knew that their journey was far from over and that more adventures awaited them in the magical world they had come to love.

Back in Cartoon Land, they were greeted by their friends, who were eager to hear about their latest adventure. Timmy and Bingo shared their discovery with excitement, showing off the amulet and journal. "This is incredible!" one of their friends said, marveling at the artifact.

"You two are always finding amazing things." Timmy and Bingo smiled, feeling proud of their latest achievement. "We couldn't have done it without your support," Timmy said, grateful for the encouragement of his friends.

As they settled into their routine, Timmy and Bingo continued to explore Cartoon Land, always on the lookout for new adventures. The amulet and journal became valuable tools in their quest to uncover the secrets of their magical world. "I'm looking forward to seeing what else we can discover," Timmy said, his eyes filled with excitement. Bingo agreed, his tail wagging eagerly. "Here's to many more adventures," Bingo said, his voice brimming with enthusiasm. Timmy and Bingo knew that their journey was just beginning and that the future held countless possibilities for exploration and discovery.

The adventures in Cartoon Land had shown Timmy and Bingo the magic of exploration and the joy of uncovering new mysteries. They embraced each day with a sense of wonder and curiosity, eager to see what lay beyond the horizon. "Every day is a new adventure," Timmy said, looking out over the colorful world he had come to love. Bingo nodded in agreement, his eyes shining with excitement. "And I wouldn't have it any other way," Bingo said, his voice filled with happiness. Timmy and Bingo knew that their adventures would continue, and they looked forward to every new challenge and discovery with open hearts and eager spirits.

CHAPTER 10: CARTOONS AND ME FOREVER

Timmy sat on his favorite grassy hill, the one that overlooked his beloved Cartoon Land. The memories of his incredible adventure still danced vividly in his mind. He thought about the amazing characters he had met, the challenges he had faced, and the magical places he had explored. "Wow, what an adventure that was!" Timmy said to himself, feeling a warm sense of nostalgia. He looked out over the horizon, imagining the colorful world beyond. "I'll never forget the incredible journey I had," he said, a smile spreading across his face. The adventures he had experienced in Cartoon Land were something he would treasure forever.

The impact of cartoons on Timmy's life was profound and lasting. Before his adventure, cartoons were simply a source of entertainment. Now, they represented a world of possibilities, imagination, and adventure. "Cartoons are more than just shows," Timmy realized with a sense of wonder. They had taught him about bravery, friendship, and the magic of believing in oneself. "They've shown me that imagination has no limits," Timmy thought, feeling grateful for the lessons he had learned. The magic of cartoons had woven itself into the very fabric of his life.

Timmy's love for cartoons grew even stronger after his journey through Cartoon Land. He watched his favorite shows with a newfound appreciation, seeing them through the lens of his own adventures. "I see so much more in cartoons now," Timmy said, his eyes shining with excitement. Each character and storyline now felt like a personal connection, a piece of his own story. "It's like I'm part of their world," he said, feeling a deep sense of belonging. His heart swelled with joy as he thought about the countless cartoons that had become a cherished part of his life.

The lessons Timmy learned from his time in Cartoon Land were invaluable. He had discovered the importance of courage, kindness, and teamwork. "Facing challenges head-on and helping others is what truly matters," Timmy reflected. He realized that every adventure, no matter how big or small, had something to teach him. "Life is full of opportunities to learn and grow," Timmy said, feeling inspired. The wisdom gained from his journey would guide him through all the adventures that lay ahead.

Timmy's belief that cartoons were more than just shows became a core part of his identity. He saw them as a gateway to endless imagination and possibility. "Cartoons are a reflection of our dreams and desires," Timmy said, understanding their deeper significance. They weren't just animated stories; they were a celebration of creativity and wonder. "They remind us that anything is possible if we believe in ourselves," Timmy added. His experiences had shown him that the magic of cartoons was a powerful force for inspiration and joy.

Looking forward, Timmy was excited about the prospect of more adventures, whether real or imagined. He knew that his journey through Cartoon Land was just the beginning of his exploration. "There's so much more out there to discover," Timmy said, feeling eager and hopeful. He looked forward to new stories, new characters, and new challenges that would come his way. "Every day is a chance to experience something new," Timmy thought, his heart brimming with anticipation. He was ready to embrace whatever adventures awaited him, knowing that the spirit of exploration would always be with him.

The idea that cartoons and Timmy would always be connected filled him with a sense of happiness and contentment. He knew that the magic of Cartoon Land would remain a cherished part of his life. "Cartoons have become a part of who I am," Timmy said, feeling a deep connection to his experiences. They represented the joy of imagination and the wonder of possibility. "No matter where life takes me, I'll always carry a piece of Cartoon Land with me," Timmy said, smiling. The bond he shared with the world of cartoons was a lasting treasure that would continue to inspire him.

As Timmy grew older, his love for cartoons remained as strong as ever. He shared his passion with friends and family, introducing them to the magic that had so profoundly touched his life. "You've got to see this show!" he would say, excited to share his favorite cartoons. His enthusiasm was contagious, spreading the joy of animated adventures to those around him. "Cartoons have a way of bringing people together," Timmy said, appreciating the connections they helped him make. The world of cartoons continued to be a source of joy and inspiration for everyone he met.

Timmy often found himself reminiscing about his adventures in Cartoon Land, reliving the moments of excitement and wonder. "Remember when we explored the Candy Mountains?" he would say, sharing stories with a twinkle in his eye. The memories were like a treasure trove of joy, each one a reminder of the magic he had experienced. "Those were the best times," Timmy said, feeling a deep sense of nostalgia. The adventures were a part of his personal history, a collection of moments that had shaped who he was.

The lessons Timmy had learned from his time in Cartoon Land became guiding principles in his life. He approached challenges with courage, faced problems with creativity, and embraced every opportunity with enthusiasm. "Every challenge is a chance to learn and grow," Timmy would say, applying the wisdom he had gained. His experiences had taught him to see the world with wonder and to believe in the magic of possibilities. "Life is an adventure," Timmy said, embracing the lessons that had become a part of his daily life.

Timmy's appreciation for cartoons evolved into a lifelong passion that shaped his interests and pursuits. He began creating his own stories and drawings, inspired by the animated worlds he loved. "I want to create the same magic that inspired me," Timmy said, excited to share his own creativity. His imagination flourished as he explored new ways to bring his ideas to life. "Cartoons have shown me the power of creativity," Timmy said, feeling empowered by his newfound skills. His love for cartoons had sparked a desire to contribute to the world of animation.

The connection between Timmy and Cartoon Land remained a source of comfort and joy throughout his life. Whenever he felt overwhelmed or needed a break, he would revisit the magical world in his imagination. "Cartoons are my escape and my inspiration," Timmy said, finding solace in the world he cherished. The adventures he had experienced continued to provide a sense of wonder and excitement. "I can always count on cartoons to brighten my day," Timmy said, grateful for the enduring magic. The bond he shared with Cartoon Land was a cherished part of his life.

Timmy's journey through Cartoon Land had taught him that the magic of cartoons was a reflection of his own dreams and desires. He understood that the world of animation was a mirror of the creativity and imagination within him. "Cartoons are a celebration of what we can achieve," Timmy said, appreciating their deeper meaning. They represented the limitless potential of imagination and the joy of exploring new possibilities. "They remind us that we are capable of amazing things," Timmy said, feeling inspired by his experiences.

As Timmy looked back on his adventures, he felt a deep sense of gratitude for the experiences that had shaped his life. "I'm so thankful for the magical world of Cartoon Land," he said, reflecting on the joy it had brought him. The adventures had been a source of inspiration, teaching him valuable lessons about bravery, friendship, and creativity. "I've learned so much from my time there," Timmy said, feeling grateful for the wisdom he had gained. The memories of Cartoon Land were a cherished part of his heart, a reminder of the magic that had touched his life.

Timmy's future adventures, whether in the real world or his imagination, were something he looked forward to with excitement. "I can't wait to see where my next adventure will take me," he said, feeling eager for what was to come. The magic of Cartoon Land had inspired him to embrace every new experience with curiosity and wonder. "There's a whole world out there to explore," Timmy said, looking forward to the possibilities. His adventures had ignited a passion for exploration and discovery that would guide him throughout his life.

The idea that cartoons and Timmy would always be connected gave him a sense of comfort and joy. "Cartoons will always be a part of me," he said, feeling a deep connection to the magical world. The bond between Timmy and Cartoon Land was a lasting treasure, a reminder of the adventures and lessons that had shaped his life. "I'll always carry a piece of that magic with me," Timmy said, smiling as he thought about his experiences. The world of cartoons had become an integral part of who he was, a source of inspiration and happiness.

As Timmy grew older, he continued to share the magic of cartoons with others, spreading the joy and wonder he had experienced. He introduced new generations to the enchanting world of animation, sharing the stories and characters that had touched his heart. "Cartoons have a way of bringing people together," he said, excited to share his love for animation. The magic of Cartoon Land had inspired him to create and connect, leaving a lasting impact on those around him. "I'm grateful for the adventures I've had," Timmy said, feeling a deep sense of fulfillment.

Timmy's love for cartoons remained a guiding light throughout his life, shaping his interests and passions. He pursued his dreams with the same enthusiasm and creativity that had inspired him in Cartoon Land. "Cartoons have taught me to believe in myself," Timmy said, embracing the lessons he had learned. The magic of animation continued to be a source of inspiration and joy, guiding him through every adventure. "I'll always cherish the connection I have with Cartoon Land," Timmy said, feeling a deep sense of gratitude.

The adventures in Cartoon Land had shown Timmy that the magic of cartoons was a reflection of the imagination within him. "Cartoons remind us of the possibilities that lie within us," he said, appreciating their deeper significance. The creativity and wonder he had experienced continued to inspire him to explore new ideas and pursue his dreams. "There's always more to discover and create," Timmy said, feeling excited for the future. The bond between him and Cartoon Land was a source of endless inspiration and joy.

Timmy's experiences in Cartoon Land had left an indelible mark on his heart, shaping the person he had become. "The adventures I had there will always be a part of me," he said, feeling a deep sense of nostalgia. The magic of animation had inspired him to embrace every challenge with creativity and courage. "I'm grateful for the lessons I've learned and the joy I've experienced," Timmy said, reflecting on his journey. The world of cartoons had become a cherished part of his life, a source of endless inspiration and happiness.

As Timmy looked back on his adventures, he felt a profound sense of fulfillment and joy. "The magic of Cartoon Land has enriched my life in so many ways," he said, feeling grateful for the experiences he had. The lessons learned and the memories made had shaped his perspective and inspired him to embrace the magic of imagination. "I'll always carry the spirit of Cartoon Land with me," Timmy said, smiling as he thought about his adventures. The bond he shared with the world of cartoons was a lasting treasure, a reminder of the magic that had touched his life.

Timmy's future was filled with endless possibilities, and he looked forward to embracing every new adventure with excitement. "I can't wait to see what the future holds," he said, feeling eager for the journey ahead. The magic of Cartoon Land had taught him to approach life with wonder and enthusiasm. "Every day is a chance to create and explore," Timmy said, feeling inspired by the lessons he had learned. His adventures had ignited a passion for discovery that would guide him throughout his life.

Don't miss out!

Visit the website below and you can sign up to receive emails whenever LEONARD KISAU publishes a new book. There's no charge and no obligation.

https://books2read.com/r/B-A-KLGKC-VFGZE

Connecting independent readers to independent writers.

Also by LEONARD KISAU

1
Best Online Ventures in 2024
Raising Girls
Sandy Beaches of Africa
Cartoons & Me

About the Author

Leonard Kisau is a devoted husband, father of four daughters, and a passionate writer who draws inspiration from his personal experiences to share stories that resonate with parents and families.

Read more at https://www.familymedia.com.